HEART AILMENTS

Explains the revolutionary vitamin E therapy which, when combined with dietetic changes, can restore damaged hearts to greatly improved function.

Hawthorne, ST rengthens the heart muscles

Dandelion Tea For wateR Retention) Odem

if take Lecithin Step up your calcium intake defieiency in calcium leads to cramps

HEART AILMENTS

Natrum Sulphate

For water Retention (oedema)

or

Buchu Juniper.

Page 27 Lecithin

1tsp night & morn

Prepared and produced by the Editorial Committee
of Science of Life Books

Take VE capsules daily

1 tsp night
& morning
Lecithin ~~cheaped~~ tbspd
~~granules~~

~~eat~~ eat enough protein .

Avoid Sugar whiteflour & other
carbohydrates
Take more exercise
Cut down on stress

SCIENCE OF LIFE BOOKS
11 Munro Street, Port Melbourne, Victoria 3207

Twelfth Edition
(completely revised and reset) 1971
Sixth Impression 1984

Registered at the G.P.O., Sydney, for transmission through the post as a book.

National Library of Australia card number
and ISBN 0 909911 38 X

Printed in Great Britain by
Richard Clay (The Chaucer Press) Ltd,
Bungay, Suffolk

Contents

Contents (continued)

Introduction

No disease is more common or more deadly than heart disease, in one of its varied forms.

Every year in Australia almost half of the deaths are due to diseases of the heart and blood vessels (cardiovascular disease).

Over 50,000 people die of these ailments in Australia every year!

That is approximately 1,000 every week, or 4,000 per month.

The road safety authorities are shocked because 3,000 people are killed on the road every year, but more cardiovascular cases die *every month*, and most of it is preventable.

If this death rate is maintained, it means that nearly every second person alive in Australia today is doomed to die of heart disease or a "stroke".

In other words some 5,000,000 people now living in Australia are doomed to die of heart trouble or hypertension.

The position is much the same in Britain and the U.S.A. According to a round table conference of the leading heart specialists of America held in December, 1949, there are in the vicinity of 15,000,000 heart sufferers in the U.S.A.

These specialists have estimated that 800,000 Americans contract heart disease every year and each year approximately 650,000 Americans die of it.

These figures are alarming. You will naturally ask, why heart disease? Is there something organically weak about the human heart in comparison with the other organs?

No. On the contrary, the heart is a notoriously strong organ. In fact, it is the most powerful muscular organ in the body. On and on it must beat — 72 times a minute, 4,320 beats per hour, 37,843,200 per year!

And the heart performs that amazing task for 50, 60, 70, 80, or 100 years or more.

The Heart — An Astounding Organ

The quantity of blood pumped by the heart varies from hour to hour. Even while we rest, the heart expels from 2½ to 4 ounces of blood from each ventricle with every contraction.

If you multiply this figure by 70, which is the average number of contractions per minute, you find that the output of blood pumped by the heart is about 4 quarts for both ventricles per minute — which is 60 gallons per hour, or 1,440 gallons per day!

To carry this mathematical exercise further and multiply the above figure by the days in the year, we get a figure bordering on the astronomical.

And this prodigious task is performed by a sturdy muscular mechanism slightly larger than a closed fist!

In terms of weight, there is certainly something astonishing about a small fist-sized organ that pumps over 11 tons of blood through an adult human body every 24 hours. ELEVEN TONS!

This fact is probably the most staggering of all the amazing facts of the human body.

Those who conclude from the foregoing facts and figures that the rising incidence of heart failure is due to this organ breaking down under constant strain are completely wrong.

The average physical worker whose heart each working day works twice, three times and four times as hard as that of the sedentary worker or housewife, *does not add seriously to the ranks of heart cases.*

The average man doing hard physical work has the best record, from the point of view of heart disease, of all the professions and avocations.

Strain is Not the Important Factor in Heart Disease

It is most important to know that heart disease was not always Killer No. 1.

One hundred years ago it ran *sixth* among the fatal

diseases of man. Sixty years ago it ran *third*. Today it is easily first.

Why is this? The usual explanation is that it is due to the increasing tempo of life — "the pace that kills".

Undoubtedly this is a factor, but by no means the most important factor, in giving rise to the high incidence of heart disease.

Sir Maurice Cassidy, the heart specialist, has put it on record that from his observations there are more heart ailments among men and women who had led relatively easy lives, insulated from the stresses and strains of life, than among those who lead the strenuous life.

The Fundamental Cause of Heart Disease

The real answer to the question: Why have heart ailments increased so alarmingly in the last 100 years when most other diseases have been greatly reduced in incidence? — was not answered until 1948, when the Shute Foundation for Medical Research, of Canada, provided the answer.

The answer to the problem, briefly, is this: The basic cause of the alarming increase of heart disease is due to the refining of flour, a practice which began about 90 years ago and has increased with the years.

When flour is refined two vital elements are removed — vitamin E and the B complex vitamins. These vitamins are only to be found in the germ cell and the husk of the grain, respectively.

The reason why flour is "refined" was due to the discovery that the germ cell of wheat contains an oil which sent flour rancid after it had been stored for about three or four months.

Remove the germ cells from the wheat with the husk and the flour would keep indefinitely. Thus treated, white flour could be sent to the ends of the earth without the danger of rancidity. The refining of flour, therefore, became the universal commercial practice.

It seemed the logical and most economical way of handling and storing flour, the most basic food in the diet of man.

But in their ignorance of vitamins, the millers dealt the health of civilized nations a mortal blow. The researches of the Shute Foundation have proved beyond doubt that—

(1) In removing the germ cell from wheat they also removed the richest known source of vitamin E, *the muscle vitamin*, which is essential for the maintenance of the vital heart muscle.

(2) In removing the husk from wheat they also removed the B group of vitamins — some 12 of them, which are essential to the nerve health of human beings.

And so it is that the white flour tradition has for nearly 100 years slowly, systematically, and increasingly starved the people of their main source of vitamin E and the B group of vitamins.

And so it is that, as a result of that long and systematic starvation, the most universal diseases today are (1) the breakdown of the powerful heart muscle and the subsequent crop of heart diseases — with one person in three dying of it.

(2) The appalling crop of nervous disorders which have characterized the last half century as the most neurotic era in the world's history. Nearly half of all hospital cases today are mental cases. Every other bed in U.S.A. hospitals is now occupied by a mental patient.

Vitamin E Repairs Heart Muscle

In 1935, while practising obstetrics in London, Canada, Dr. Evan Shute started using E on women who had suffered involuntary miscarriages.

He became convinced that the vitamin had an antagonistic action against estrogen, a hormone produced by the ovaries, which causes rhythmic contractions of the womb.

Mightn't this hormone cause dislodgment of a new life,

resulting in abortion? And wasn't it reasonable to suppose that vitamin E prevented this by neutralising estrogen?

During the summer of 1945, Floyd Skelton, medical student at Western Ontario, wanted a research project.

Shute suggested that he investigate the E-estrogen antagonism. Skelton agreed and started injecting dogs with estrogens.

Soon he noted something strange; blood vessels under the dogs' skin broke down. But when the animals were given E, the purple patches disappeared. Skelton reported this to Shute at an opportune moment.

In a London hospital, a friend of Shute's — Dr. Arthur Vogelsang — had a difficult patient, a 67-year-old man with hypertensive heart disease.

The patient was scheduled for surgery, but his condition was so poor that the surgeon was afraid to operate.

Kidneys were limping badly; fluids were causing gross swelling of legs. Rupture of blood vessels made large purple patches — and it was this that caught their interest.

E had cleared up such haemorrhages in dogs. What about man? Skelton calculated the amount of vitamin E required to get results.

Each day, the old man took massive doses. On the fifth day, Vogelsang was making routine rounds of the hospital. The patient's bed was empty. The old man was helping floor nurses with trays!

The patient reported that he hadn't felt better in years. Breathlessness was gone, and so was the leg swelling.

He announced proudly that he had done more work that morning than in several years.

Vogelsang and Shute, unprepared for this turn of events, started reading all available data on E. Besides its stimulating effect on muscles, E exerted some mysterious beneficial effect on blood vessels.

Also, muscles starved of E required a lot of oxygen — several times the amount required by healthy muscle.

Vogelsang and Shute reasoned that E's stimulating effect on blood vessels would have direct action on the heart itself.

This same stimulating effect would account for improved kidney function; and E's ability to cut oxygen requirements would minimize breathlessness.

Thus, the two men theorized their way through the problem. They were reasonably sure that the vitamin could do no harm — the body would simply discard any excess quantities it did not want.

Patient No. 2 was Dr. Shute's mother, a 71-year-old lady who had suffered stabbing anginal pains.

For fear of bringing on an attack, she avoided exercise; her arms and legs were waterlogged. After five days on E, swelling was gone and pains had disappeared.

Brother Wilfrid Shute, practising in Guelph, started using vitamin E in his own practice. In the three years that have elapsed since Case No. 1 was treated, the three-man team has used vitamin E on some 4,000 heart patients. (*Note:* Written in 1948.)

One of the commonest forms of heart disease is that which accompanies hypertension — high blood pressure.

This means that the heart must work harder to push blood through the circulatory system. It may, in time, simply work itself to death.

Coronary occlusion is another form of heart disease. In this, a clot forms on an artery in the heart, grows larger, finally blocks the flow of blood.

A fifth of the people to whom this happens die within a few hours. In others, scar tissue forms in the damaged area, cutting heart efficiency.

Rheumatic heart disease is a third form. In this some microbe as yet unidentified attacks the heart, injuring valves, destroying muscle tissue. The organ may have to labour several times as hard to accomplish a given amount of work as it did before injury.

A fourth form is caused by hardening of heart arteries. They become smaller and less elastic, thereby reducing the heart's food supply. The starved muscle reacts by forming scar tissue, which further cuts the capacity of the organ.

For the most part, laymen think of angina pectoris as a disease in itself. Actually, it is a *symptom* which may announce the presence of any of the conditions mentioned above.

Stabbing pains frequently indicate that the heart muscle isn't getting enough blood.

Vitamin E has been used for all these disorders by Drs. Shute and Vogelsang.

Amazing Benefit from Vitamin E

Of all patients treated to date, some 80 per cent. get amazing benefit, most of them losing all the usual symptoms.

Look at some of the patients. One man was a wheelchair invalid. Even sustained conversation brought on sharp anginal pains.

Massive doses of E got him out of his wheel chair. Recently, he fished all day, then played bridge until midnight. Next day, he played nine holes of golf!

A 52-year-old musician suffered attacks of coronary thrombosis over a five-year period. He started taking E in July, 1945, and hasn't spent a day in bed since.

Another man, 26, had a siege of rheumatic fever while a youngster. Now he is working in a foundry. Another patient, 71 years old, was prey to anginal pains at the slightest exertion. Now he is doing heavy work in a tannery.

On the basis of these cases — and hundreds like them —. Wilfrid Shute states bluntly: "Vitamin E is the most effective known factor in the treatment of heart disease, and certainly the safest.

"The percentage of cases which show improvement is high — 80 per cent. The degree of improvement, even in the worst cases, is often marked."

Best results recorded thus far, the Canadian physicians claim, have been obtained with anginal symptoms, with early coronary thrombosis, and in cases with early failure.

Results obtained so far seem impressive. What, then, are the objections? Critical physicians complain that the Shutes and Vogelsang have not used "controls" — that is, have not treated one group of patients by traditional methods, while treating a second group with E.

Such procedure would give a basis for comparing older methods with the new one.

To this objection, Evan Shute retorts: "We have the records of a century of medical practice to indicate the course of heart disease under standard treatment." Wilfrid Shute, who has treated 2,000 patients with E, affirms that private practitioners are in no position to do "controlled" experiments.

Secondly, physicians complain about the ever-recurring medical bugaboo: publicity. The E treatment has been publicized in Canadian newspapers and American news magazines.

Vogelsang replies that his group was in no position to stop such publication since the stories covered talks given in open medical meetings and reports in medical publications.

A third criticism is that electro-cardiograms — tracings of heart-action patterns — show little change soon after E treatment.

Vogelsang replies that some electro-cardiograms *do* show significant changes.

And that in cases where there are no changes, he is more impressed by reactions of the patient than by reactions in a strip of photo film.

The American Medical Association sums up the case of the critics: "Far too often there has been over-emphasis in the press on research too fresh from the laboratory to permit evaluation.

"The reported discovery of almost-miraculous powers of Vitamin E needs careful evaluation and confirmation, because the substance has already been investigated by many competent clinicians and found wanting."

Yet in the two years that have elapsed since this discovery was announced, no such critical reports have appeared in medical journals.

On the other hand, there has been published a wealth of data all supporting the Shute-Vogelsang contention.

Since E is the most common of all vitamins — being

present in the germ of grains, leafy vegetables, root vegetables — how could heart disease trace to a shortage of the substance in normal diet?

The Canadian physicians reply that we have made an almost-systematic effort to remove it from foods.

Bread, they point out, is our main staple, yet we remove most of the E-carrying germ from white flour. In fruit — apples, for example — it is present in peel and core, which are usually discarded. It appears in the peel of potatoes, which we throw away.

Many investigators contend that we are more deficient in E than in any other vitamin.

The Tragic Sequence of Vitamin E Deficiency

To this lack they attribute many of the vague aches and pains that beset us; and they see a definite connection between lack of vitamin E and widespread circulatory disorders.

In a host of other disease conditions where inadequate blood supply is the basic factor, such as thrombosis and phlebitis, chronic leg ulcers, Buerger's disease, even early gangrene, vitamin E has proved remarkably effective.

In their own field, the Shutes and Vogelsang note that heart disease is almost unknown among primitive peoples — until they start eating civilized man's food.

Further, they emphasize that in 1910 — before our national diet had become too refined — heart disease was the fourth cause of death instead of the first, as it is today; and that the *rate* of heart deaths is up 250 per cent. in this period.

Many people attempt to explain this away by noting that early in the twentieth century, when the life span was shorter, people didn't live long enough to get heart disease.

But cold fact lends little support to this idea. We may regard heart disease as an ailment of the aged, but it is the third cause of death in the five-to-24 age group, and the top killer thereafter.

The evidence, then, seems to add up to the fact that we may all be gravely short of vitamin E.

If the Canadian physicians are correct in their beliefs, the prevalence of heart disease may be simply an expression of this want.

3,300 U.S. Doctors Using Vitamin E for Heart Cases

The original opposition developed before doctors had tried the treatment themselves. But now, a single pharmaceutical company can point to 3,300 medical men in the U.S. who are using vitamin E for heart disease.

No longer are there on the one side three dedicated advocates, on the other, a mass of vocal critics. Evan Shute puts his case as follows:

"It is hard to imagine that what vitamin E does to clots in superficial vessels, it cannot also do for the vessels of the heart. The controversy can be settled with ease.

"All that is necessary is for an unprejudiced cardiac clinic to treat alternate patients by our methods and by traditional methods.

"The results will tell the story quickly. If we are wrong, it will be simple to prove it. If we are right, everyone should know about it."

The fact that the Shute discovery is right is conclusively proved by the results — 80 per cent. of heart cases are amazingly improved, if by "improved" we mean that all the old distressing symptoms of breathlessness, angina attacks, exhaustion, and invalidity are no longer present after a few months' treatment with massive doses of vitamin E.

Please note that the article in the *Coronet Magazine* was printed in 1948.

Since then the splendid promise which vitamin E therapy gave in the early years of clinical experiment has been confirmed in thousands of cases and by medical practitioners in several parts of the world.

In addition, research workers followed up some

hundreds of serious heart cases, selected at random, which
had passed through the Shute Foundation some two years
previously. Approximately 73 per cent. of these cases
reported no return of symptoms.

A Remarkable Survey of 250 Cases

In the hope of ascertaining the real picture of the then
condition of the early patients treated by alpha tocopherol
(vitamin E), representatives of the Shute Foundation made
a personal survey of the first 250 of the early patients who
could be personally reached in a radius of 200 miles of the
Shute Foundation for Medical Research which is
established in London, Canada — all of them patients
treated before the end of 1947.

The average time which had elapsed since these 250
heart cases were treated was 27 months, the time since
treatment finished varying from 18 to 22 months. One
hundred and fifty-seven were males and 93 females.

Where patients had died their histories were traced
through surviving relatives or friends.

The method was by house-to-house-to-office-or factory-
canvass, and a careful interrogation followed by a further
medical examination.

Two years later, 204 of the 250 patients were still alive,
and, curiously enough, 204 were still taking alpha
tocopherol (vitamin E) regularly as prescribed.

Ninety-six of these patients had seen other physicians
before consulting the Shute Foundation, and a very large
number had passed through the hands of the leading
cardiologists of Canada and U.S.A.

Many came to the Shute Institute for Medical Research
in extremis — that is to say, in the last stages.

Of those who died was one who died within 24 hours of
visiting the Institute. Others died within the first three
weeks of receiving alpha tocopherol therapy (vitamin
E) — *within which time alpha tocopherol rarely takes hold.*

Most of the patients treated by the Shute Foundation
had previously been under reputable heart specialists, and

had been taking nitro-glycerine, digitalis, or other heart
drugs.

No dietetic changes were insisted upon when the
patients were first treated. This decision was made, not to
disparage the important effects of diet on the heart
condition, but so that the effects of vitamin E could be
judged exclusively on its own merits.

On the question of diet, the Shute Foundation makes
this observation:

"Diabetics who are on dietary and insulin management
are aware that *both* are needed and that each assists the
other, but are apt to ascribe most of their benefits to
insulin. *And yet insulin is always given with a dietary
adjunct!*" Why not with heart cases?

Here then are the results of the examination of 250
patients treated with vitamin E and followed up some two
years after passing through the Shute Foundation:

Angina Cases

		%
A.	Complete Relief of Clinical Signs and Symptoms	60
B.	Marked Improvement	16
C.	Little or No Improvement	16
D.	Deaths	8

Coronary Heart Disease

		%
A.	Complete Relief of Clinical Signs and Symptoms	53
B.	Marked Improvement	17
C.	Little or No Improvement	15
D.	Deaths	15

A summary of the foregoing results is as follows:

	%
Complete Relief of All Signs and Symptoms	56.5
Marked Improvement	16.5
Little or No Improvement	15.5
Deaths	11.5

The percentage of those relieved of all distressing heart
symptoms or very much improved is 73 per cent.

This is remarkably high when it is considered that the heart cases which go to the Shute Foundation for treatment are generally the worst cases in the last stages.

If all heart cases from the first symptom — i.e., the first time they felt obliged to consult a doctor or a heart specialist — were put on vitamin E therapy, the curative results would be much higher.

Two other factors conspire to keep the percentage of greatly improved cases much lower than it should be:

(1) The refusal of most patients to seriously follow dietetic instructions and

(2) The inconsistency with which people dose themselves with vitamin E, some on the ground of its expense and some because of negligence.

And yet in spite of these factors, 73 per cent. were restored to virtually normal health and activity in 12 weeks!

Drs. A.L. Pascoe and Wilfrid E. Shute make the following comments on the foregoing tables:

"It is to be remembered that the patients in our series were not the mild cases, but the desperate cases who sought the help of vitamin E as a last resort, the real coronary cripples . . .

"The small group of deaths in the series is especially striking. There were only 26 deaths, an annual death rate of 5.6 per cent.!

"When it is realized that 96 per cent. of the Shute Foundation's patients had been treated for better or for worse for years before we saw them, this becomes an even more significant figure.

"If only we had had a chance to rescue all of such hearts, rather than just what was left of them!

"Compared to what results are achieved by such orthodox therapy as bed rest and some such drugs as digitalis, the benefits derived from vitamin E represent an incalculable relief of human misery and despair."

How Vitamin E Works

How does vitamin E bring about this amazing change for the better?

It does it in a number of ways:

(1) Primarily, vitamin E is the "muscle vitamin". It dilates the capillary blood vessels, enabling the blood to flow more freely into muscle tissue, thus strengthening the muscle tissue and carrying blood more freely to the network of nerves throughout it.

(2) The significance of this will be more apparent when it is remembered that the heart is primarily a piece of muscle tissue — and the most important muscle in the body.

Vitamin E — or rather, the alpha tocopherol in it — revitalizes and strengthens heart muscle that has deteriorated and restores it to more normal function. Its lesions are healed, and the heart is "made over".

(3) But vitamin E does much more than that. It decreases the oxygen requirement of muscle by over 40 per cent. Thus pain and breathlessness disappear and the sufferer is no longer exhausted by the slightest exertion.

As Professors Houchin and Mattill have pointed out: "This oxygen conserving mechanism in coronary heart disease is obviously of the greatest importance and probably explains the complete disappearance of angina pectoris in most patients on an adequate dosage of alpha tocopherol.

"It is really equivalent, as far as oxygenation is concerned, to increasing the blood supply to the heart — which is, of course, the fundamental corrective needed for proper cardiac function."

(4) Vitamin E also possesses an anti-thrombin quality. That is to say, it prevents the clotting of blood in arteries and veins. But it does more, it dissolves blood clots. These qualities reduce the incidence of thrombosis.

(5) To quote Dr. Evan Shute: "It acts somehow upon both old fibrous heart tissue, as shown by Steinberg, of Rochester, and Burgess & Pritchard, of Montreal, and also upon the formation of new scar tissue."

(6) It improves the whole circulatory mechanism of the body in general and the heart in particular.

"Vitamin E" (alpha tocopherol), to quote Professors Hickman and Harris, "is the most versatile and active of all the vitamins."

It is not surprising, therefore, that drastic changes for the worse develop in so many millions of human beings who are systematically starved of it. And it is equally not surprising that amazing changes for the better take place once vitamin E is systematically taken into the body.

Dr. Evan Shute on Vitamin E

Dr. Evan Shute, the principal of the Shute Foundation for Medical Research, enlarging on the way vitamin E works, has said:

"These functions of vitamin E, all of them extensively confirmed in animal experimentation and human clinical work, make it the most valuable ally the cardiologist has yet found in the treatment of heart disease. It has no rivals. No other substance has this array of needful properties. Vitamin E then becomes the first safe factor which can be given to patients suffering from the results of a clot in a coronary artery.

"There has been and still is no treatment at all for this type of case, except two mildly useful drugs, which can be administered with great peril to the already precarious patient.

"Vitamin E replaces 'rest and reassurance', which have no authentic basis, with real help to the damaged, laboring heart itself.

"It is the key both to the prevention and treatment of all those conditions in which a lack of blood supply due to thickened or blocked blood vessels or a lack of oxygen is a major factor of the whole story of the disease. As I have said, it has no rivals.

"No pharmacologist or cardiologist can suggest another substance with all the powers and properties of this vitamin. God made it unique and we ignore it at our peril.

Work Declared World Famous

"This work is world famous. Some 96 medical papers, not including our own, have already been written in its support. How many does one need to win his case?

"Our work seems to have been the source of Ochsner's studies on the prevention of post-operative clotting by the use of vitamin E, of the work of many Italian workers on heart disease, of Professor Boyd's (of the University of Manchester) published treatment of intermittent claudication (Buerger's disease) and with phlebitis.

160 Medical Men Patients in Institute

"We have over 160 medical men as personal patients at our institute. We know of many more who are taking it on their own. Presumably what is good enough for them is good enough for their patients. Early this month one appeared who had been a successful surgeon in California. After a heart attack he had been given vitamin E by his doctor. He merely came to us for regulation of his dosage. He used these words to me: 'Everybody is using it for the treatment of heart disease in California!' — A pleasant but slight exaggeration, perhaps.

"There is much animal experimentation to show that vitamin E may be the key to the control of hardening of the arteries. I cannot help but recall the words of the great pathologist, Gideon Wells, under whom I studied pathology for 15 months, who told me that the man who discovered the prevention and treatment of arteriosclerosis had found the key to eternal youth. A man is as old or as young as his arteries.

"I would, if I had time, give you in detail the results of some of these experiments. I would like to tell you about the workers who showed that the deposits of cholesterol in the wall of the arteries in rabbits force-fed with cholesterol could be prevented by vitamin E.

Over 10,000 Patients Treated

"We have now personally treated over 10,000 cardio-vascular patients. My great regret is that circumstances today prevent me from showing you some of our hundreds of coloured photographs of these people. I wonder how many people realize that this is many times the number seen in a comparable time elsewhere.

"We are no longer reporting on our first ten cases. We are reporting to you on the conclusions derived from thousands. It is an investigation that Canadians and Canada should be proud of, for in this at least they lead the world."

What Vitamin E Can Improve It Can Also Prevent!

The truth is of the greatest important to those many thousands of people who have not yet suffered a heart attack but who have had warnings that their hearts are heading for trouble.

These people should begin taking vitamin E at once. Their dosage need only be two-thirds of the dosage required by angina cases namely 200 mgms daily but sufficiently high to help PREVENT such a deadly thing as a coronary occlusion — which is often fatal — happening to them.

And for those people who are still in possession of sound hearts, with no symptoms whatever of heart trouble, it is a wise precaution for everybody past the 30 years mark to begin supplying the body with the vitamin E which they do not get in their daily food supply.

They should begin the practice of taking 100 milligrams per day which is low cost insurance against heart disease in any of its lethal or crippling forms. From 40 to 60 years, 150 mgms. daily is advisable, and after 60 years 200 mgms. daily.

Other Curative Factors

There are three other vitally important factors in the salvaging of damaged hearts in addition to vitamin E. These three factors are:

(1) A special diet drawn up on the principles recommended by three famous nutritional scientists — Professor McCollum, Gayelord Hauser, and Dr. Howard Hay.

The nutritional principles for heart cases reduces those forms of protein which add to the viscosity (or glueyness) of the blood stream, and which give the heart a much heavier task as a pumping mechanism.

(2) The addition of B complex vitamins. Exhaustive experiments have proved that in laboratory animals the heart is the first organ to suffer when the B group of vitamins are withheld.

The B complex vitamins were automatically removed from the food of man, along with vitamin E, when he began the suicidal practice of refining flour.

Gayelord Hauser has written: "Scientists who have studied the drastic results of vitamin B deficiency on the heart, estimate that this deficiency plays an important part in the cause of heart disease."

The B group of vitamins are essential for sound nerves, and as one medical authority has pointed out, "chronic nervous tension can overwork the heart muscle to a dangerous degree — that is, by making it work faster and harder. It is this factor which puts added stress on the heart muscle."

(3) In cases of heart weakness due to rheumatic fever, vitamin C is an important curative factor. "Heart infections", says Gayelord Hauser, "are produced in experimental animals only when they lack this vitamin."

What You Should Know About The Heart

Whilst the heart sufferer does not require to understand all the intricate mechanism of the heart, he should know a little about it.

The three important parts of the heart's structure are:

(1) The muscle that contracts and pumps the blood;

(2) The valves through which the blood enters and leaves the heart;

3. The blood vessels (coronary arteries) that carry

oxygen and nourishment to the heart muscle.

The heart consists of four chambers — the left and right ventricle, and the left and right auricle, also called left and right atrium — atrium means the first chamber — The walls of all four chambers consist of muscle.

It is vitally important that he understands *why* and *how* the circulatory mechanism in general and the heart in particular becomes silted up.

Spend a few minutes studying the diagrams of the heart on pages 30 to 31.

You will notice a network of arteries on the outside of the heart. This is an anterior view. There is also a network of arteries, veins, and tiny blood capillaries throughout the heart muscle.

The arteries which you can see in the diagram (and a network of arteries which you cannot see) are called *coronary arteries.*

These coronary arteries feed the heart muscle. They carry blood to all portions of the heart muscle.

Now turn to the illustration on page 32 and note how these arteries are silted up, making it difficult for the blood to flow through.

What are these deposits in the coronary arteries and how do they come about?

These deposits are partly uric acid deposits — acid urates, xanthine, hypoxanthine, creatine, and others.

They are the end products of wrong feeding, of excess protein (meat and eggs chiefly) white bread, condiments, pickled vegetables, corned meat, toasted and processed breakfast cereals, strong tea and coffee, sugar, jam, processed desserts, sausage meats, pastry and confectionery, sweetened foods, etc.

Meat and eggs are valuable protein foods eaten in moderation. For heart cases, however, protein foods must be reduced to about four ounces a day.

But the other foods mentioned are dead foods, "foodless" foods — devitalized, demineralized, and devitaminized — and no person with a bad heart, should EVER eat them. No healthy person should eat them either, if he hopes to retain his health.

How Arteries Become Silted Up

The net result of such a diet upsets the acid-alkaline balance of the blood stream and increases the uric acid waste. What is not eliminated by the kidneys is gradually deposited on the walls of the arteries and veins.

Mixed with this uric acid residue is the cholesterol from animal fats.

Post mortems show these deposits to be almost as hard as slate. The slow silting-up of the whole circulatory mechanism may take 40, 50, 60, or 70 years before it brings about the inevitable degeneracy of the circulatory mechanism.

Lined with this mineralised deposit, the blood vessels lose their elasticity. A condition popularly known as "hardening of the arteries" develops.

And, of course, this silting-up process, with the consequent loss of elasticity in the vasculatory (or circulatory) mechanism, goes on right throughout the entire body and the brain.

This process may finally lead to blockages in an artery of the brain, causing first a ruptured blood vessel, and then a "stroke". It is this process which frequently causes thrombosis in the arteries or veins of the legs.

Consider the added burden placed on the heart when the blood vessels of the body are silted up. It is still obliged to pump the entire blood supply through these half-closed pipes. But to do so it must pump much harder. Is it any wonder that the heart muscle so frequently breaks down under the strain; more especially when the blood in addition, is thick and gluey?

What Cholesterol Is

Cholesterol is a constituent of all animal fats and oils. It is insoluble in water; is important in metabolism and can be activated to form vitamin D.

There is much talk nowadays about cholesterol, in relation to heart ailments.

A survey of a group of patients who died of coronary

thrombosis, conducted in America and reported in the *American Heart Journal,* vol. 39, 1950, showed that the cholesterol content of their coronary arteries was four times that of normal patients.

Cholesterol is, however, essential to health. It is vital to nerve tissues and is partly responsible for the semi-solid consistency of the living cells. It is also needed for certain hormones and the bile salts.

It is dangerous to eliminate *all* fatty foods from the diet, because of a fear that cholesterol will silt up the blood vessels. Moreover, some fatty foods are essential in the diet, to permit the proper assimilation of the fat-soluble vitamins A, D, E F and K; without which, health is impossible.

The threat from cholesterol is largely due to man's continual tampering with natural foods (with the object of commercial gain).

What can be done to prevent cholesterol being deposited in the blood vessels, with disastrous results to health?

Nature supplies the answer with lecithin (pronounced less-i-thin), which has the property of emulsifying cholesterol and reducing it to tiny droplets that are readily assimilated and do not form harmful deposits to clog the veins and arteries.

Lecithin is contained in whole grain cereals, but is removed in the milling process and is not therefore available to consumers of white bread and white flour products.

Lecithin is richly contained in unprocessed cereal and vegetable oils such as safflower seed oil, sunflower seed oil, soya bean oil, peanut oil, wheatgerm oil, etc. Lecithin is an excellent source of the two B complex vitamins, choline and inositol. Most animal foods are extremely poor sources of lecithin.

Lecithin helps the body to absorb vitamin A and it improves the body's utilization of vitamin E.

Many people find difficulty in taking vegetable or cereal oils. Capsules now provide in a convenient form, a concentrated dosage of lecithin, in the form of safflower seed oil, sunflower seed oil, etc.

The Effect of Refined Sugar

Foods containing significant amounts of refined sugar are under attack for their detrimental effect upon health. In her book *Let's Eat Right to Keep Fit*, Adelle Davis, eminent American nutritional scientist, stated that the American diet "has become largely one of sugar". Refined sugar is added to so many foods nowadays, e.g., cereals, cakes, biscuits, pies, desserts, ice cream, soft drinks, puddings, sauces, custards, jellies, canned fruits, soups and vegetables, infant foods, sweets, "instant" mixes, etc., that the daily diet is virtually deluged with sugar.

Dr. J. Yudkin, Professor of Nutrition and Dietetics, University of London, who has conducted considerable research into the dietary habits of the peoples of forty-one nations, considers that a high intake of refined sugar is a major cause of heart disease and hardening of the arteries.

Australia's consumption of refined sugar is one of the highest in the world.

The Cause of Coronary Occlusion and Angina

Is it any wonder that the silting-up process continues to such an extent that a small blood clot is blocked in the small coronary arteries of the heart, giving rise to the dreaded, often fatal, heart attack, medically known as "coronary occlusion" or "coronary thrombosis"?

Is it any wonder that under physical strain, such as hurrying for a train, or walking uphill, or under some emotional stress, the narrowed, silted arteries of the heart, having lost their capacity to dilate (expand), cannot supply the heart muscle with the increased blood and oxygen it requires, and the victim suffers a most acute and terrifying attack of pain beneath the breast-bone, across the upper part of the chest, and down the left arm?

This attack is called *angina pectoris* and is due to the failure on the part of the coronary arteries to supply the heart muscle with sufficient oxygen.

A heart attack can be brought about by eating a heavy meal. Indeed, most of them occur after a heavy meal. The heart has to pump more blood to digest it. The heavy meal is often the "last straw".

Immediately following a coronary occlusion (i.e. the blockage of the supply of blood to a portion of the heart muscle) the part of the heart affected is without oxygen, toxic wastes accumulate, and the patient experiences severe pain.

The portion of the heart muscle deprived of its nourishment and oxygen dies, and scar tissue gradually forms in the part affected (see page 33).

Small, new blood vessels from nearby arterial branches open up, and help to take the load off the now defunct artery, but this takes time.

But because the heart is weakened by the death of a portion of its muscular wall, little strain can be put upon it. If too much is demanded of the heart in this weakened state, it may fail altogether or the wall may rupture, hence the need for bed-rest.

A Thickened, Gluey Blood Stream

There is another important aspect of the heart problem which arises out of the old dietetic tradition. It is this:

The excess protein food eaten by most people gives rise to a blood stream of high viscosity. In simpler language, this means that it causes the blood to become thicker, sticky or gluey.

This factor again puts an added strain on the pumping mechanism – the heart. It stands to reason that the greater the thickness, or viscosity, of the blood, the greater the blood pressure.

(Remember that high blood pressure and heart trouble are often associated. They are really two different manifestations of the same thing. And some people have both. It is then called hypertension.)

Even normal, healthy blood is about five times thicker than water. The more viscous and sticky a fluid is, the more resistant it is to flow, and the greater the pressure required

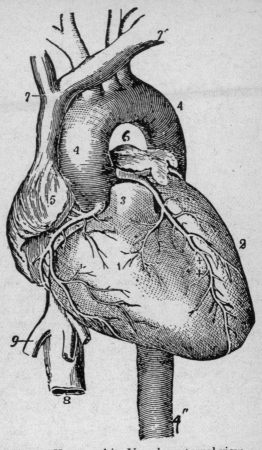

The Human Heart and its Vessels, external view.
1, right ventricle; 2, left ventricle; 3, root of the pulmonary
artery cut short; 4, 4' and 4'', the aorta; 5, right auricle; 6,
left auricle; 7, veins which unite to form the vena cava
superior; 8, inferior vena cava; 9, hepatic vein, plus
coronary arteries.

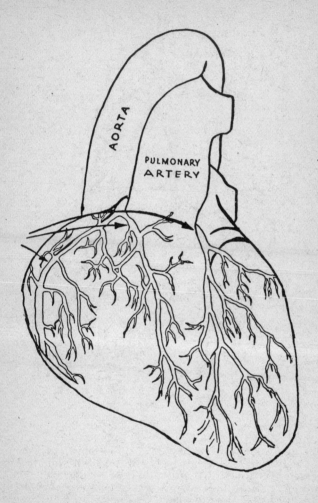

An illustration of the distribution of the coronary arteries. They carry blood to all portions of the heart muscle.

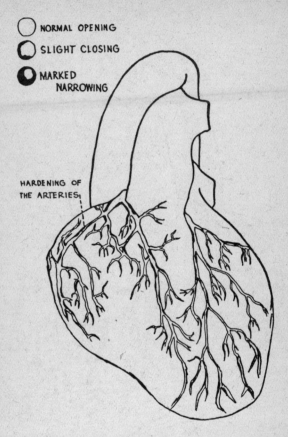

The above illustration shows the silting up process in the coronary arteries which supply the heart with blood. This process is called arteriosclerosis, or hardening of the arteries. It is in these narrowed blood vessels that a blood clot blocks the flow of blood, causing coronary occlusion, with angina pectoris pains, commonly referred to as a "heart attack".

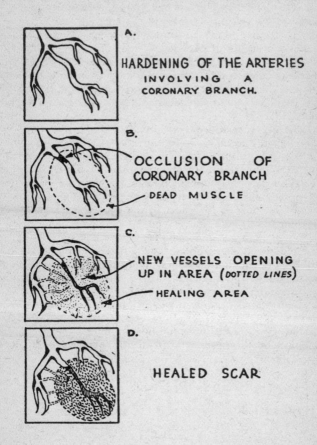

A.

HARDENING OF THE ARTERIES
INVOLVING A
CORONARY BRANCH.

B.

OCCLUSION OF
CORONARY BRANCH

DEAD MUSCLE

C.

NEW VESSELS OPENING
UP IN AREA (DOTTED LINES)

HEALING AREA

D.

HEALED SCAR

Illustrating the stages of healing of the heart wall, following
an occlusion of a small branch of a coronary artery.

to force it through a narrow tube such as a blood vessel. It follows that a thickened, gluey bloodstream being pumped through partially obstructed blood vessels imposes a tremendous task upon the heart.

Let us see what Dr. Howard Hay has to say on this important matter of viscosity:

"Do not be shocked if I tell you that there is just one cause for this condition, for this is the simple truth, even though there is great discussion and disputing among the heads of the scientific world to-day as to what is the real cause.

"In every case, yes, *every case*, blood pressure comes from an increasing viscosity, thickness, stickiness, glueyness of the life current, and this condition comes always from the over-saturation with one ingredient of our daily ration.

"You may easily guess that this is protein, one or several of the various proteids, for they all possess this property of glueyness, such as the white of the egg exhibits, and this is an almost pure protein.

"Now, it is just possible that this increasing viscosity of the blood stream would not occur without a disturbance in the balance of the tissue salts, or an absence, or paucity, of vitamins, for there are seeming exceptions to this rule that excess of proteins leads inevitably to this one condition.

"But this is begging the question, for in the absence of an excess of proteins in the body, high blood pressure would be unlikely. So too would degeneration of the kidneys or the heart which often accompany high blood pressure.

The Toll Taken by Excess Protein

"In a close observation of many hundreds of cases of blood pressure, hardening arteries, degenerating kidneys, dilating hearts, in a private and sanatorium practice covering the past thirty years, I have not seen one single exception to the rule that an excess of protein is behind every case, the average being well over ten times as much

protein as Chittenden says is necessary to repair body
waste, and many of these cases admitted an amount of
protein generally in the form of meat, that comprised thirty
or forty times the Chittenden standard."

Chittenden proved by figures and experiments that have
never since been successfully controverted that the human
body requires but one gramme of nitrogen for every 30
pounds of body weight, or for a man of 150 pounds four
ounces of lean steak for an entire day, or the equivalent in
other protein-bearing foods.

"An excess of protein means that if one's exercise and
physical work are not sufficient to oxidise or burn up this
excess fully, it forms protein acids, such as uric acid, acid
urates, and others.

"All these acids are very irritating and act as clinkers in
the grate, or as the proverbial monkey wrench in the
machinery of the body."

What Eight Scientists Discovered

The Hay Theory of viscosity has its backing in a medical
report issued in 1950 by an eight-man team of scientists
from California University after two years' research.

These scientists claimed that a hard waxy-white substance called cholesterol is present in animal fats and eggs.

Led by Dr. John Gofman, the scientists report three
main discoveries:

(1) When people were given food rich in cholesterol
some individuals automatically built up gluey substances in
their blood.

(2) Swellings which formed inside "hardening" arteries,
giving rise to the dangerous blood clots, contained large
quantities of the "glue". They seemed to arise as a direct
result of its irritating action.

(3) Examination of patients who suffered sudden heart
seizures showed that their blood was specially rich in the
"glue". When they were put on a diet deficient in
cholesterol the "glue" rapidly thinned down.

These discoveries also help to explain why seizures and

strokes often run in families. The experiments also throw light on the reason why men are so much more susceptible than women to heart ailments in middle age. The scientists found that men usually have far more of the "glue" in their blood, due no doubt, to the fact that the average man eats more meat and other protein food than the average woman.

Vitamin E Prevents Blood Clots

The following cable from U.S. appeared in the Australian Press in July, 1954:

A team of Tulane University surgeons has suggested the possibility of heading off potentially-fatal blood clots by means of a "relatively simple" laboratory test.

They said the test offered promise of predicting, with a great deal of certainty, which patients are likely to develop blood clots following operation or as the result of certain other conditions like heart disease.

They declared that for such patients there is some hope that the administration of a chemical that is naturally present in blood may help prevent the formation of clots.

The Tulane surgeons also said that there had been an increase in the number of cases of, and deaths from, blood clots of the veins in recent years.

They advanced the theory that this increase may be due to the almost routine use of so-called "antibiotic" drugs like penicillin in combating infection in hospital patients. They explained that such drugs — valuable in fighting germs — also tend to make the blood coagulate more easily, thus favoring the formation of clots in some cases.

The surgeons in a report to the 13th Congress of the International Society of Surgery, said that apparently a chemical called "alpha tocopherol" — the active therapeutic factor in vitamin E and a normal constituent of blood — is at least one of the factors responsible for preventing clot formation.

This vitamin, they said, could be given by mouth to patients believed likely to have a clot.

"He's Had a Coronary"

We quote from *Your Heart and Vitamin E*, by Dr. Evan Shute:

"The report, 'He's had a coronary!' conveys word to everyone of a sudden heart attack, often immediately fatal, often permanently crippling if the patient survives.

"If he lives, he exists only to wait in apprehension of another 'attack'. Everyone knows that, like strokes, these tend to repeat.

"It should therefore be immediately stated that there are two major types of coronary disease and that the drastic kind described above is a novel and distinctive product of the twentieth century. It is this kind that is probably preventable, *but if it has occurred, it should be treated at once with vitamin E in massive dosage. Nothing else offers comparable hope or relief* . . .

"Alpha tocopherol dissolves the clot or thrombosis partially or completely — *if it is of recent occurrence.* Thus it may even prevent death of part of the heart area otherwise doomed.

"Vitamin E decreases the oxygen need of the whole zone of injury and preserves much of its normal structure and function.

"It returns the zone of anoxia (deficiency of oxygen) towards normal and helps the whole injured heart to work more efficiently. Proof of this is the more rapid and more complete recovery of heart power in people adequately treated from the start with vitamin E.

"Recurred attacks tend to be prevented by the continuous use of alpha tocopherol *in full dosage.*

"Unfortunately, immediate treatment with alpha tocopherol is denied to many patients as yet. This is one of the cruellest results of the slow medical acceptance of vitamin E treatment for heart disease.

"When a coronary patient survives the initial attack, even if he displays a good deal of heart impairment, he is still an excellent subject for vitamin E treatment.

"One other point must be stressed here. Normally, the danger of a clot forming on the inner wall at the site of damage and so lying loosely in the chamber of the heart is great. *With vitamin E this danger is diminished and usually absent.*

"Embolism, as the detachment of a clot is called, is very rare in our experience.

"This paragraph should be of utmost interest to every male and to most females.

"Coronary thrombosis kills nearly half the males who die over the age of 45.

"Only two cases of clotting in the coronary artery were described prior to 1900 in spite of the great interest in and careful examination of coronary arteries at autopsy for decades before that time.

"Clearly this is a disease of the twentieth century, unrelated, therefore, to coronary arteriosclerosis (hardening of the arteries), an old and well-recognised disease.

"The relationship in time between the beginning and rapid increase of this disease and the deprivation of alpha tocopherol in our diet is too obvious to need stress here . . .

"Providing blood pressure is normal and there is no old rheumatic damage to the heart, a good 80 per cent. of heart cases respond to an adequate dose of a properly labelled product — taken faithfully every day as long as the patient wishes to remain well and alive."

Further Evidence of Vitamin E in Preventing Thrombosis

Medical Thesis, published in Paris, Number 471, 1951, quotes a physician as saying he has found vitamin E and calcium useful for preventing blood clots after surgery.

Dr. R. Bauer, writing in *Wiene Klinisch Wochenschrift*, a German publication, volume 31, page 552, 1951, says Dr. Ochsner's method (which used vitamin E) can be used successfully in reducing to one tenth the usual incidence of thrombosis and should perhaps be used to decrease the danger of clot in coronary thrombosis.

Drs. M. Reifferscheid and P. Matis, writing in *Medizinische Welt*, Germany, volume 20, page 1168, 1951, announce they have found vitamin E to be definitely protective against vascular clotting. They found that large daily doses (500 to 600 milligrams) were necessary. They describe five cases of diabetic gangrene, nine cases of Raynard's disease (a gangrous condition), seven cases of Dupuytren's contracture (contraction of tissues under the skin of the palm) and 14 cases of hemorrhagic (bleeding) diseases all yielded to treatment with vitamin E.

Dr. W.E. Crump and E.F. Heiskell, writing in the *Texas State Journal of Medicine*, volume 11, 1952, agree that the use of the regular anti-coagulants for routine prevention of clotting diseases in patients after operations is too dangerous for general use. In most cases where these medicines are used, as many patients die of hemorrhage as might have died of clots and 16 per cent. of other cases develop non-fatal bleeding complications.

When vitamin E was used as treatment by these physicians no bleeding occurred and only minor side reactions were noticed. When cases of phlebitis occurred during treatment, they were mild and had no complications. There were no lung clots, fatal or non fatal, in patients being treated with vitamin E.

Dr. Terrel Speed, commenting on these statements, says, "considerable evidence is accumulating to substantiate the value of this therapy. However, I have gradually expanded its use and now it is used routinely in essentially the same group of cases mentioned by the authors. If the promising preliminary results are borne out, relative protection against one of the most feared complications of surgery will have been obtained."

Two German physicians, S. Schmid, writing in *Wiene Klinish Wochenschrift*, volume 64, and H. Wagner, writing in *Aertzliche Wochenschrift*, volume 7, page 248, 1952, say they have achieved good results in treating thrombosis with vitamin E.

The foregoing evidence is most significant, both as to the prevention and cure of coronary occlusions, post-operative thrombosis, and clots in the cerebral arteries causing stroke.

Angina Pectoris

Before we proceed further, let us briefly examine the various types of heart ailment.

Angina Pectoris really means sharp pain in the chest; "breast-pang", as it is sometimes called.

The term is applied to a group of symptoms rather than to a definite disorder, though the condition is usually associated with disease of the heart, especially of certain of the arteries by which the heart itself is nourished, or with disease of the aorta, the great blood vessel which leads directly out of the heart.

When an attack comes on, the symptoms are most alarming. There is agonising pain in the region of the breast bone, with a sense of painful choking constriction in the chest.

The attacks are usually brought on by various causes, such as the hasty eating of a meal, the eating of too much food, sudden over-exertion, intense excitement or emotion of any kind. This is why many sufferers imagine they have indigestion and take indigestion medicines.

Constriction of the arteries around the heart is the physiological cause of the attack.

The overall cause of the condition, as we have seen, is due to the systematic deficiency of vitamin E over the years, together with an excess of cholesterol and uric acid waste in the blood.

Coronary Artery Disease

This is a narrowing or occlusion of the coronary arteries, generally due to their having hardened. It results in insufficient blood reaching the muscular tissue of the heart (myocardial ischemia) with consequent damage and impairment of the heart's action.

A coronary thrombosis means that a blood clot (thrombus) has obstructed a coronary artery supplying blood to the heart, leading to a disordered heart action.

A coronary occlusion means that the artery is closed or shut off.

Hypertrophy

Hypertrophy of the heart: This condition is often developed by people submitting the heart to abnormal strain, such as athletics. The heart becomes enlarged.

Back of this condition, however, there is usually a history of wrong feeding and the slow poisoning of the blood stream.

One authority says: "Where there is hypertrophy, it means that in attempting to carry on its full activities under a condition of great strain, one or both of the lower ventricles of the heart have become enlarged to enable it to cope with the abnormal task."

Some people with enlarged hearts suffer little inconvenience, but with others the condition is accompanied by dizziness, headache and head noises.

Dilatation of the heart: This is usually a development of hypertrophy. It means that the compensating factors of heart enlargement have deteriorated.

Dilatation is a condition of decided weakness and danger. Shortness of breath after the slightest exertion, disturbed sleep, more or less continual discomfort in the region of the heart, palpitation, etc., are its accompanying symptoms.

Endocarditis and Myocarditis

Endocarditis: This is a condition in which there is inflammation of the membrane which lines the cavities of the heart. The disease may be acute, or chronic, and is positively associated with a highly toxic condition of the system. Endocarditis usually leads to definite disease of the heart.

Myocarditis: This is the term used to denote inflammation of the muscular tissue of the heart. The condition may be acute or chronic and leads to progressive degeneration of the heart muscle with greater or lesser impairment of heart action.

Pericarditis: This is the term applied to inflammation of the pericardium, or membranous sac in which the heart is enclosed.

Anaemia and the Heart

Blood is red because of floating red discs called red blood cells. They contain a substance (haemoglobin) that carries oxygen from the lungs to the heart muscle and other body tissues. One may think of them as rail-road cars.

They carry their product (oxygen) from the point of supply (lungs) to the consumer (heart muscle).

If these red cells become fewer and fewer for any one of many causes, a condition called *anaemia* is present.

This means that even though there is an adequate supply of oxygen in the lungs, there are not enough rail-road cars (red cells) to carry it to the consumer (heart muscle).

If such a state is allowed to continue, the heart suffers.

Valvular Diseases

Valvular disease of the heart may be of various kinds, ranging in degree from very serious to comparatively slight.

In valvular heart disease the valves which shut off the heart chambers one from another, or which shut off the great arteries leading from the heart itself, have become either too large or too small, thus interfering with the proper passage of the blood to and from the heart, with greater or lesser disturbance of bodily function.

The greater predisposing factor towards the setting up of valvular heart disease is inflammation of the heart lining (endocarditis); and this is often the outcome of rheumatic fever, scarlet fever, etc., plus a blood stream systematically poisoned over a period of years — a heart muscle starved of vitamin E.

Congestive Heart Failure

When the heart muscle becomes weakened, overfatigued, or "strained" and can no longer meet the demands made upon it, a condition known as congestive heart failure exists.

For example, in cases of high blood pressure in which the heart is enlarged to the limit of its coronary blood supply, the cardiac reserve is used up, and the heart is no longer an efficient pump, the following things happen as a result. The left ventricle is tired and can no longer completely empty the pumping chamber.

A small amount of blood remains in the ventricle after contraction.

The left auricle contracts, but because of the blood already in the ventricle it cannot completely empty itself. Blood backs up and produces congestion in the lungs.

The right ventricle cannot empty, the left auricle cannot empty, and the blood backs up in the tissues.

Because of the back pressure in the veins carrying blood right back to the heart, fluid from the blood leaks out into the tissues and causes swelling. The ankles and legs are the first to show this swelling known as dropsy or oedema.

The patient with congestive heart failure complains of shortness of breath and he may develop an irritating cough because of the congestion in his lungs. The veins of his neck may stand out, and his ankles become swollen.

All these symptoms may result from a tired and inefficient central pumping system.

Other Heart Ailments

Mitral Stenosis: A constriction or narrowing of the mitral valve between the left auricle and the left ventricle.

Bradycardia: A slowness of the heartbeat with a rhythm of less than fifty beats a minute.

Tachycardia: Excessive rapidity of the heart's action, with a rhythem exceeding one hundred beats a minute.

Early Symptoms of Heart Trouble

The following are the symptoms that you may be heading for heart trouble:

(1) Breathlessness upon such exertions as going up stairs or steps, hurrying for a train, etc. And/or a feeling of fatigue or exhaustion following any undue exertion.

(2) Discomfort in sleeping. A desire to prop oneself up in bed so that one may breathe more freely.

(3) Giddiness or light-headedness.

(4) A sensation of dull pressure on the breastbone, extending to the left shoulder and down the left arm. In some cases only the left shoulder and arm may be affected.

(5) Pains in the chest after meals, or upon exertion. These are often taken for indigestion pains, when they are angina symptoms.

A person may experience no more than one or two of those symptoms, but he should take them as definite warnings that more serious heart trouble is ahead if prompt steps are not taken to:

(a) Strengthen the heart muscle with a moderate amount of vitamin E daily;

(b) Improve the general nervous system and the nerves of the heart with B complex vitamin tablets daily;

(c) Reduce the viscosity of the blood by eating much less meat and egg proteins;

(d) Reduce the deposit of cholesterol in the arteries by cutting down on all fat foods;

(e) Cut down on sugary and sweetened foods and drinks.

(f) Build up the general health by sound nutrition as advocated further on in this book.

More Serious Symptoms of Heart Trouble

The following are symptoms of heart trouble of a more advanced nature:

(1) Breathlessness upon exertion and a sense of fatigue or exhaustion after it.

(2) Racing heart (Tachycardia).

(3) Pain in the region of the breastbone. It may be slight, but in a "heart attack", it is usually agonising and alarming, spreading down the left arm, and accompanied by a painful choking constriction in the chest, and a state of collapse. These are the symptoms of the dreaded *angina pectoris*, commonly referred to as a "heart attack".

(4) Swellings in the ankles and feet. This dropsical condition is called oedema. The tissues of the ankles and feet become saturated with fluid. This is a sign of congestive heart failure.

(5) In congestive heart failure fluid can also seep into the lungs, causing shortness of breath, congestion of the lungs and an irritating cough.

Why the Usual Treatment Fails

Now, if you are a sufferer from some heart ailment it won't help you a scrap to be told that you suffer from, say, endocarditis instead of say, myocarditis.

These shades of difference in heart ailments interest the medical profession, but they are of little significance to the sufferer.

Why do we say that? *Because all these fine distinctions in heart disaffection are merely different manifestations of the same causation.*

If you are interested in removing the trouble you will naturally look to the factors that have *caused* it, and having once ascertained them, you will discontinue those practices or habits. That is the simple, commonsense thing to do.

But how does the average orthodox doctor proceed to treat the heart sufferer? Chiefly by rest and the use of drugs.

The most dangerous weapon in the armoury of orthodox medicine is its reliance upon drugs to effect a cure, whether it be the heart or any other organ.

The specialist who uses digitalis to slow the rapid heart, adrenalin to accelerate a slow heart, or amyl nitrate to relax a tense heart, or trinitrite to dilate a restricted artery, has succeeded at best in stopping a symptom, temporarily, by imposing great additional strains upon an already over-loaded organ and its controls.

The following extract from Dr. W.H. Gordon's book on the heart — Dr. Gordon is one of America's leading cardiologists — is typical of the advice given to heart patients by orthodox medicine so far as heart disease is concerned:

"Nitroglycerin tablets, amyl nitrite perles, alcohol, and certain other drugs seem to dilate or cause the small coronary branches to relax, making the small vessels larger.

"People who have angina pectoris from effort are frequently able to prevent their pain by placing a nitroglycerin tablet under the tongue just before doing a task which they know from experience will result in pain.

"For example, if a man must walk up a hill from the trolley every night when he comes from work, and he knows that if he walks up the hill he will have to stop a time or two because of pain, he may put a nitroglycerin tablet under his tongue as he gets off the trolley and go up the hill without pain.

"However, a better idea would be for the individual to move to another site, where there is no hill, or to go home by another route. Many people's lives have been made more comfortable by such compromises.

"A drink or two of brandy or whisky each day may be helpful in causing the arteries to dilate and is certainly not forbidden if the patient would like it.

"Following a coronary thrombosis, drugs that produce dilatation of the small blood channels are given to speed the healing process."

The foregoing advice speaks for itself. As emergency therapy it may serve its purpose, but such treatment with drugs and alcohol as a general thing, inevitably makes the heart condition worse.

Treatment on the lines indicated by Dr. W.H. Gordon — which is fairly general — *has never been known to give any substantial or permanent improvement to a bad heart condition.*

Drugs and Heart Ailments

The over-all effects of drugs may be definitely harmful for the heart. They fail to take into account the natural law that "action and reaction are opposite and equal".

That is to say, the drug that gives artificial stimulation to a feeble heart today will do it at the price of greater enfeeblement tomorrow. That dangerous policy leads to greater quantities of drugs to get the same stimulation, and enfeeblement to the point of death the moment the drugs are left off.

Many medical scientists now agree (1) that no heart ailment was ever permanently cured by drugs; (2) that cure can only be effected by fundamental changes in the body's nutrition in general and by vitamin E in particular.

Sir William Osler, one-time Regius Professor of Medicine at Oxford University, was fond of quoting Voltaire's indictment of drugs and druggers:

"We put drugs, of which we know little, into bodies which we know less, to cure diseases, of which we know nothing at all."

If you are on drugs now, give them up gradually, not suddenly. As your blood stream improves, so will you be able finally to dispense with the taking of drugs altogether.

Even the B.M.A. Warns on Drugs

Dr. Ulric Williams, Ch.B. (Edinburgh), on the question of drugging for health, wrote:

"We indulge our perverted appetites with refined, denatured and adulterated food in almost any quantity and combination. We ignore almost all the commonsense requirements with regard to rest and exercise, sunlight, fresh air, water, clothing and posture. Physical and mental deterioration are the inevitable accompaniments.

"Yet when Nature graciously warns us of the danger by the appearance of inconvenient symptoms, we look upon these as diseases, and insult the delicate structure of the body with deadly poisons in a variety of forms in the hope of regaining our health.

"A remarkable paradox, especially as these drugs are administered to suppress symptoms that are the result of faulty living."

Importance of the B Vitamins

As we saw earlier in this little book, the B vitamins — of which there are about 12 — are lost from the so-called "staff of life", together with vitamin E, when flour is refined.

They are destroyed when wheat and other cereals are turned into flaked breakfast "foods", first by blowing the grain out with steam and then toasting the flakes in an oven.

The general effect of this process is to produce a popular breakfast cereal — crisp and tasty, but depleted of many nutrients.

The public does not pause to consider that the tastiness is due almost entirely to the addition of sugar and milk, and that as an article of diet, perfectly good grain has been turned into foodless pap — its vitamin and mineral content practically destroyed. The milk probably has the greatest food value.

If poultry or pigs were fed solely on corn flakes, they would very likely die, yet they flourish on corn.

The vitamins destroyed in the refining of flour and the wicked processing of breakfast foods are the B complex group, which are vitally important to the whole nervous organization of the human body and brain.

No wonder we are a race of neurotics, flying to every drug to dull and deaden our aches and pains and dull our jumpy nerves into temporary subjection.

The effect of this systematic starvation of the B complex vitamins upon the heart is important.

A new generation has grown up in the last 40 or 50 years with a new cardiac phenomenon — the nervy, erratic heart.

All heart patients, therefore, regardless of the type of heart ailment from which they suffer, should make a point of redressing this B vitamin deficiency in the most forthright way — by making wheatgerm, yeast, and molasses daily articles of diet and B complex vitamin tablets a routine daily practice.

The B group of vitamins are essential for sound nerves, and as one medical authority has pointed out, "chronic nervous tension can overwork the heart muscle to a dangerous degree — that is, by making it work faster and harder. It is this factor which puts added stress on the heart muscle."

The taking of B complex tablets, which contain thiamine to help regulate the heart's rhythmic beat, with vitamin E, is becoming routine practice, and with increasingly beneficial results.

What About Exercise?

You have no doubt already been counselled by your doctor to take things very quietly, not to run for trains, or wheel barrow-loads of earth up hills, etc.

While rest is important and all strenuous exercise must be discontinued, some light exercise is important to the restoration of the heart to a normal condition. Walking is generally recommended, plus a good skin brush after your bath each day.

But most exercise should be avoided until you are on the road to recovery, and then gradually increased, but always kept within your cardiac reserve.

The Electrocardiograph is Often Misleading

To quote Dr. W.H. Gordon, in his work on *Heart Disease*, "the electrocardiograph is an important and useful diagnostic aid, but it is not the wonder apparatus many believe it to be.

"Unfortunately, many persons believe that the one and only way to make a correct diagnosis of heart disease is through its use.

"This is not true. Heart disease may exist even though the electrocardiogram is normal, and conversely, there may be abnormal changes in the electrocardiogram that are not the result of heart disease.

"Loud murmurs caused by scarred and leaking valves may be present although the electrocardiogram is normal.

"It should be realised, therefore, that this laboratory aid, like all others, has its limitations, and all interpretations of tracings should be made only by physicians who are well aware of these limitations.

"The electrocardiograph does not reveal the strength of heart muscles or the probable outcome in any specific case, although it is helpful in many ways."

Seven Causes of Heart Ailments Summarized

Now let us summarize the seven basic causes of the alarming incidence of heart disease:

(1) The systematic starvation of the heart muscle of vitamin E — the muscle vitamin — resulting in the gradual weakening of the most important muscle, with the hardest task and the greatest responsibility, in the human body.

(2) A serious deficiency of B complex vitamins in the diet, causing chronic nervous tension which overworks the heart.

(3) A dietetic tradition which gives rise to an excess of uric acid waste and cholesterol — a constituent of all animal fats in the blood stream, causing wastes, in the form of urates, and a hard slatey substance, to silt up the arterial and venous mechanism, thus increasing the work of the heart in pumping the blood, causing blood pressure and blockages in the flow of blood, i.e. coronary occlusion or "stroke" (if in the brain).

(4) An excess amount of protein — especially meat and eggs — in the diet, causing a thickened, sticky or viscous blood stream, which also leaves its deposit on the arterial walls and puts an added strain on the pumping mechanism — the heart.

(5) Too much sugary and sweetened food and drink.

(6) A dietetic tradition which perpetuates the evil practice of eating heavy meals of several courses, and diluting the ill-selected contents of the much-abused digestive system with tea, coffee, beer, wines or spirits.

As blood is required for the digestion of meals, the ultimate burden of over-eating falls back upon the poor old heart.

(7) A sedentary life, in which the average business man is far too busy to find time for daily exercise to keep his muscles firm and the heart in good physical condition. The result is that the heart becomes encased in fatty tissue, it loses its tone and the general physical condition slumps. A "heart attack" merely indicates one vulnerable link in the armour. It is inactivity that kills.

The foregoing are the seven fundamental causes of heart disease — the western world's No. 1 killer.

The Seven Remedial Principles

Once we understand the *causes* of a human ailment, we are half-way to curing it.

By reversing the seven causes and by applying the curative principles *consistently*, 80 out of every 100 heart sufferers can not only rid themselves of distressing — indeed, alarming — heart symptoms, and the serious limitations that accompany them, but can gradually regain a high standard of health they may not have enjoyed for many years.

Here are the seven steps to achieve these objectives:

(1) Supply the heart muscle with vitamin E, the lack of which has been largely responsible for its deterioration and its disease.

(2) Take three B complex vitamin tablets daily to restore nerve health in general and reduce the nervous tension of the heart in particular. One or two vitamin C (250 mgm.) tablets should also be taken to build robust, healthy walls for the veins and arteries, enabling them to cope with the flow of blood without weakening.

Vitamin C also helps to build strong connective tissue, and destroys bacteria that invade the bloodstream.

(3) Arrange one's diet so that it consists of vital foods. Cut out the "foodless" foods which are listed, and follow (as closely as possible) the Ideal Diet for Heart Cases.

(4) Reduce the protein, sugary, and fatty foods to the minimum. Most heart cases are the better for cutting out fat meat, eggs, and animal fats. But if you are not prepared

to do that, reduce meat and eggs to one small serving each day. Substitute cheese as your main protein. It has a better protein value than meat or eggs and is rich in calcium, which is essential for the health of the bone structure and the *nerves*.

(5) Eat *less* — much less. Most heart sufferers are over-weight — a fact which puts an added strain upon the heart in pumping blood throughout a circulatory system entombed in fat.

(6) Gradually restore the body to better physical tone by moderate exercise and skin massage.

(7) Cut out cigarette smoking, which constricts the blood vessels.

Reject These Pseudo Foods

Here is a list of "foodless" foods that no heart patient should eat. These are the "foods" which create the uric acid deposits that silt up the circulatory mechanism:

White bread.

White flour products, including pies and cake.

Sugar — white or brown.

Processed breakfast foods — flaked, "puffed" or refined.

Pastry and biscuits.

Confectionery.

Excessive servings of animal fats.

Sausage meat.

Corned meat, pickled and tinned meat.

Fried foods.

Re-heated and re-cooked soups, meat and vegetables.

Pickled vegetables.

Salt, and salty foods.

Strong tea and coffee, soft drinks.

Condiments of all descriptions.

Jam.

Most packeted and tinned foods, "Instant" foods.

All "puddings", indeed all desserts other than fruit, stewed fruit, junket or yogurt.

The above "foodless foods" cause most of the ills to which the flesh is heir.

They are responsible for saturating the tissues with acid end-products and for silting up the vascular (circulatory) system with uric acid deposits and cholesterol.

They may be the cause of glandular malfunction, which slows up the whole governing mechanism of the body.

In short, the long term effect of these alleged foods is homicidal.

The wise man and woman will wipe them off the dietetic list, not only for the duration of the treatment, but for the duration of life.

Professor McCollum on Heart Disease

Professor E.V. McCollum, of Johns Hopkins University, the noted American scientist, has written:

"I have repeatedly made the statement that there is no such thing as heart disease, meaning that there is no disease which can attack the heart without first having fastened itself on some other part of the body, finally finding its way, through circulation or otherwise, to the heart muscle.

"My purpose is to try to show readers how they may lighten the burden on the heart by increasing the general health of those parts of the body that have the most influence over its condition . . .

"The speeding up of civilization is not the only cause of nervousness and hypertension.

"In the light of our understanding of the science of nutrition, we see that even a slight dietary and vitamin deficiency may wreak havoc in the nervous system, producing various and changeable symptoms throughout the body.

"A toxic condition may irritate an otherwise healthy nervous system to such a degree that the harmonious function of all the vital organs is upset — including that of the heart.

"Such toxic conditions may result from constipation, over-eating or over-indulgence of alcohol, tobacco or sweets.

"Simple indigestion, following the use of unwise food

combinations, can cause the stomach to be so inflated with gas as to press against the heart and push it out of shape.

"Such a condition, if allowed to advance to an acute degree, or if tolerated over a period of time, might prove to be very troublesome or even fatal . . .

"While learning to control your nerves and emotions, the question of proper food supply must not be overlooked. *Neither the nerves nor the heart muscles they control can be stronger than the food materials from which they are constructed.*

"These important parts of the body have to be repaired continually as they wear out. The repair parts come only from the meal table, and if a wrong selection is made, the tired, worn parts of the body have to suffer . . ."

The Meat-Eating Fallacy

Heart patients are strongly advised to eat meat, eggs and fish very sparingly — no more than a small serving two or three times a week when on the road to recovery.

As we have seen, these proteins are one of the chief factors in causing a gluey, viscous blood which puts an unfair strain on the heart and increases the tension on the arterial walls.

The tradition that meat is essential for strength is a fallacy. The British people are meat eaters by tradition.

But there are examples of physically powerful — and far healthier — people who eat meat only occasionally. One such race is the Hunzas of Northern India.

According to Sir Robert McCarrison, an eminent medical scientist who spent nine years among them, in Northern India, the flesh-abstaining natives of that locality, the Hunzas, are "an example of a race unsurpassed in perfection of physique and in freedom from disease in general, whose sole food consists of grains, vegetables and fruits, with a certain amount of milk and butter, with goats' meat only on feast days."

The Art of Eating Less

The heart sufferer should now resolve to *eat much less, eat very lightly and eat far better* — that is, select his food with more intelligence.

He must quickly learn that for damaged hearts a salad is a far, far wiser meal than meat and vegetables, followed by dessert.

He should cultivate the all-fruit-meal habit — such as two apples or three or four ripe peaches or a pound of grapes, or a dish of stewed fruit.

An all-fruit meal is a better lunch for heart sufferers than sandwiches, or a grill, or an omelette, or corned beef, fish or cold chicken.

The raw salad vegetables — grated carrot, grated beet-root, grated apple, lettuce leaves, parsley, celery sticks, tomatoes, ripe sliced bananas and sliced pears, etc., *supply the blood with most of the essential vitamins and minerals — except vitamin E, which is taken in capsule or tablet form.*

Salads and fruits *purify* the blood, *detoxicate* the system, reduce the *viscosity* (stickiness) of the blood, *and thus reduce the pressure on the pumping station, the heart.*

These three factors are fundamental to any cure or any improvement in the condition.

The heart sufferer must get rid of the erroneous notion that a salad or an all-fruit meal as *part* of his daily diet will "sap his strength".

On the contrary, his health, energy and strength will improve amazingly with sound nutrition and vitamins E and the B complex.

Just as unsound nutrition, lacking especially in vitamin E, may have been a major cause of his heart weakness, so will sound nutrition, plus vitamin E and B complex vitamins, greatly improve it.

The Body Rebuilds Itself

A most important point to remember is this:

The body — and all its parts — is constantly renewing itself.

Every day some two or three ounces of dead tissue cells — the dead tissue of bone, muscle, nerves, arterial walls, and organs — are passed out of the body.

And every day these dead tissue cells are being replaced by new cells from the protein food we eat.

If the food we eat is right — if it has sufficient protein for worn-out tissue replacement, but no more than that; if it contains the necessary vitamins and minerals for pure blood and efficient glandular and organic functioning, then it can be said that the body is slowly rebuilding itself, renewing and repairing damaged parts.

The new connective tissue for the arteries will be of a highly elastic and resilient quality, and a form of "invisible mending" will take place.

By this amazing process, nature rebuilds tissue to heal wounds, rebuilds injured parts, renews defective organs, and knits bones.

It is generally agreed by physiologists that the entire body is renewed every seven years.

No person with a diseased heart, kidneys or vascular mechanism, therefore, need despair. He can renew himself.

But if he would build soundly, if he would change a defective piece of body mechanism for a sound one, he must use sound building materials.

The great thing to remember is that the body never stands still. It is either rebuilding its cell structure or the cell structure is in process of deterioration.

In short, we are either rebuilding ourselves or destroying ourselves, in strict accord with what we eat and how we live.

By beginning today, we can be either cured or substantially better in three, six, or twelve months. By continuing on in the same reconstructive way we can — literally — be "a new man", or woman, at the end of seven years.

Ideal Diet for Heart Cases

Before Breakfast: A large glass of orange juice, lemon

juice (half water), pineapple, tomato, or apple juice. These drinks should not be sweetened with sugar.

With the fruit drink take one vitamin C tablet (250 milligram).

Breakfast: Three dessertspoons of wheat germ — with milk. You can have it with milk, by itself, or with grated apple or stewed fruit. Or you can have the stewed fruit — apricots, prunes or peaches — separately. Alternative to stewed fruit is a bunch of grapes.

With breakfast take one third of the vitamin E you are required to take daily. If the daily requirement is 300 milligrams, take 100 milligrams of vitamin E before breakfast.

The vitamin E dosage is given later in this booklet.

You can chew the tablets up with the meal — they are quite pleasant to take — or wash them down with milk. They are best assimilated at meal time.

Mid-Morning: Cup of weak tea, and slice of wholemeal bread or toast, with peanut butter, honey, marmite or vegemite.

If you must sweeten tea or fruit drinks, use honey. Honey is 100 per cent. food value and not acid forming. It contains vitamins and minerals.

If you can't accustom yourself to honey as a drink sweetener, reduce your sugar consumption considerably by taking a little less each day.

In a month or two you can educate yourself to a new taste — and like it.

The same with strong tea. Take it progressively a little weaker. Your heart needs every consideration.

A word on bread. Many people simply can't get a loaf which is wholemeal. Very well. The answer is to cut down your bread consumption to two or three slices a day.

Lunch: There are three ideal lunches: (1) Two or three apples and about 4 oz. of cheddar cheese. No bread. Cheese and apples are a perfect food combination. Try it.

(2) A large green leaf salad, with cheese, grated carrot, beetroot, grated apple, parsley, pinch of mint, sliced bananas, pears, etc. Or any happy combination of salad

vegetables or fruits in season.

(3) A plate of fruit and a glass of milk. Four ripe peaches, for example, and a glass of milk is an excellent meal for a heart sufferer. Or a pound of grapes.

With lunch take one-third the vitamin E you are required to take daily, and one B complex tablet, and one lecithin capsule.

Afternoon Tea: Your usual afternoon tea or a cup of fruit juice.

Evening Meal: If you had apples (or peaches) and cheese for lunch, now is the time to have your large salad. You can vary it no end — with an occasional slice of ham, cold meat and tomatoes, etc. In winter time, precede the salad with hot soup.

In summer time, the salad may be followed by an acceptable dessert — fruit, banana cream whip, fruit salad, or an ice cream.

By way of a dietetic change, a plate of steamed vegetables with cheese sauce.

When on the road to recovery, a little grilled meat or fish may be added — no more than twice a week.

With the evening meal take the remaining third of your daily vitamin E capsules or tablets and one B complex tablet, one vitamin C (250 mgm.) tablet, and one lecithin capsule.

Before retiring take six calcium tablets and a glass of warm milk to make sure of your calcium intake, which is essential for the relaxation of heart nerves. This will also induce sound refreshing sleep.

A Word of Warning

The heart sufferer should be warned that the foregoing somewhat sudden changes in his diet may have rather disturbing physical and psychological effects.

Nature does not adjust herself quickly, or agreeably, to sudden changes in habit.

Nature takes time to make adjustments. When the huge liner S.S. United States is travelling at 35 knots and the engines are reversed, she still travels *forward one mile* before beginning to move backward.

When nature starts to "clean house" the person concerned generally feels worse for several days.

Unfortunately, this feeling is generally interpreted to mean that the treatment is wrong — that it is doing more harm than good.

This is a mistaken idea. You know what a home is like during the process of spring cleaning.

But when the job is finished and everything is restored to its right place, the house looks "wondrous neat and clean."

So it is with the body. The dietetic changes recommended by nutritional science are comparable to a spring cleaning. We are invariably upset by it.

But if we persevere, an abiding sense of well-being takes possession of us, and finally we get well.

And once restored to health it is easy, armed with the new knowledge of nutritional science, to stay well.

Don't worry about the loss of weight that your new diet will cause. As you become sound in health, your weight will find its normal level. Meantime, loss of excess weight means a lighter burden on the heart.

The Vitamin E Dosage

The dosage recommended by the Shute Foundation for Medical Research — which has made the effects of vitamin E on the heart its special study over several years — is as follows:

Coronary Heart Disease, including coronary occlusion and thrombosis: Where the blood pressure is not higher than 160 systolic, the dosage for this type of heart condition is 300 to 500 milligrams of vitamin E daily, otherwise 200 mgms. daily for the first 4 weeks. A routine practice is that one B complex tablet is taken with vitamin E during or immediately before each meal.

To avoid danger of relapse, 300 mg. of vitamin E should be continued indefinitely, even after all heart symptoms have disappeared.

If after five weeks the heart symptoms have not disappeared, 500 mg. of vitamin E daily should be taken, or increased if necessary.

The Shute Foundation stresses the importance of treating all cases of coronary occlusion (or thrombosis) *immediately* with 500 mg. of vitamin E.

Owing to the unfortunate fact that most physicians are not yet acquainted with vitamin E therapy for cardiological cases, months, sometimes years, elapse before the patient starts on vitamin E. Had he commenced to take it immediately, his chances of recovery to better heart function would have been greatly increased.

Angina Pectoris: Where the blood pressure is not higher than 160 systolic, the daily dosage should be 300 to 500 mg. of vitamin E. If higher, start on 100 mg. daily for 4 weeks, then increase by 50 mg. daily after each 4 weeks until 300 mg. or more daily are being taken.

Hypertrophy, Endocarditis, Myocarditis, Pericarditis, Mitral Stenosis, are heart conditions which respond to 300 milligrams of vitamin E daily, *plus one vitamin A capsule, one vitamin C tablet, 250 mg., one B complex tablet, one B1 tablet (10 mg.), and one lecithin capsule, before each meal.*

Hypertensive Heart Disease — that is, heart symptoms complicated by high blood pressure:

100 mg. vitamin E daily for one month
120 mg. vitamin E daily for the second month
150 mg. vitamin E daily for the third month

Then the dosage should be lessened, maintained, or slowly increased by 20 mg. daily per month, according to the doctor's report.

To quote the Shute Foundation: "Of necessity the treatment of these cases is gradual and prolonged, but the results are very often satisfactory from the patient's standpoint. Indeed, relief of symptoms may be marked after the patient has been on 150 to 180 mg. of alpha tocopherol (vitamin E) per day for a month or so, rarely on smaller dosage, and we often do not proceed to larger doses."

Diet for Hypertension cases should be relatively salt-free on the lines set out in the dietetic section of the Science of Life booklet, *High Blood Pressure*.

One B complex tablet is now routine practice, with the vitamin E dosage, before each meal, in every form of heart disorder.

Lecithin capsules are also recommended (see page 27).

Acute Rheumatic Fever — the first attack: "If such cases are treated *immediately* with **400 mg.** of vitamin E daily, irrespective of age, all evidences of disease may disappear in as little as 3 to 7 days — at least by three to four weeks. Fever, joint symptoms and signs, tachycardia (excessive rapidity of the heart's action) will, in many a case, disappear entirely. We have had very few failures on such a schedule. — (Drs. W.E. and E.V. Shute, in *Alpha Tocopherol in Cardiovascular Disease*).

Continuing Rheumatic Fever with marked damage to the heart, with or without congestive failure, and with or without auricular fibrillation. The Shute Foundation says:

"Here is a group in which we have rarely failed to obtain definite improvement, sometimes very striking and maintained for months, in each case with reduction of heart size, usually with disappearance or better control of the congestive failure, and with apparent inactivation of the disease. However, the damage is often enormous and all such patients face constant danger from intercurrent infections or sudden cardiac failure."

Subsequent attacks of acute Rheumatic Fever in a latent case. Herein the ideal treatment is 400 mg. vitamin E daily. There are some cases in which the damage from earlier attacks is so great that the full dosage cannot be given immediately. If heart size is nearly normal and heart damage moderate or relatively slight, we try full dosage. If damage is great we give 100 mg. daily for two weeks and then cautiously try full dosage. In a few cases we must treat these patients cautiously, giving 90 mg. per day for the first four weeks, 120 mg. daily for the second four weeks, and 150 mg. for the third four weeks, with increasing dosage if or as directed." (Shute Foundation).

Cautions

In serious heart ailments, the maintenance dosage equals the therapeutic dosage, and any reduction of the vitamin E dosage can result in a serious relapse.

Inorganic iron tonics should not be taken at the same time as vitamin E. They seem to destroy the action of the alpha tocopherol and also vitamin C. Paraffin as a laxative and estrogen preparations also destroy vitamin E.

It cannot be too strongly emphasized that only the dosage indicated gets results. Attempts to get a moderate improvement with a moderate dosage invariably fail. The Shute brothers have warned that a half dosage is equal to NO DOSAGE.

It is the *alpha tocopherol* content, according to the researches of the Shute Foundation for Medical Research, which plays the fundamental part in salvaging bad hearts and restoring them to normal function.

Vitamin E is made up of alpha, gamma, beta, delta and three other tocopherols, but only *alpha tocopherol has any therapeutical value*.

On this point the famous Shute Foundation for Medical Research, which has made Vitamin E its special research for several years, has written:

"The only preparations of any value are those labelled in terms of alpha tocopherol since it is only the alpha tocopherol which has any therapeutic value. Therefore gamma, beta and delta tocopherols possess no value whatever in the treatment of cardio-vascular disease. They are inert members of the mixture of natural tocopherols which comprise vitamin E."

It is most important to use a reliable brand of vitamin E.

What To Do

Can one take vitamin E and other vitamins without a medical prescription?

Yes. There is no danger in taking vitamins in prescribed dosages because vitamins are vital food factors; they are not drugs.

What is the difference between drugs and vitamins? A very great difference. Drugs are dangerous and should only be taken under the supervision of a doctor. Practically all drugs have side-effects, some of which are a serious hazard to health. But vitamins are "food accessories", which have the power to work amazing changes for good in the body — and appalling changes for the worse if we are starved of any of them.

Are doctors using vitamin E therapy for heart cases?

Thousands of doctors in U.S.A. and Canada are, where the remarkable results have been brought home to them.

Many doctors in Australia are now introducing vitamin E therapy to their patients, and the number is destined to grow rapidly.

Most Notable Medical Advance

It should be known that the Shute Foundation for Medical Research has no commercial interest in vitamin E or in any firm that manufactures or sells it. It is a medical research foundation pure and simple, supported by public subscriptions and the fees of patients.

Many medical men are convinced that the Shute Foundation's contributions to medical science and cardio-vascular diseases will yet receive world-wide recognition as the most notable medical advance of this era.